This edition

Montague House, Lambridge St,
Bath BA1 6RX

First published 1996

Printed in Singapore

THE LITTLE BOOK OF JOKES

On quiet nights, when he is alone, Fred runs their wedding video backwards, just to watch himself walk out of the church a free man.

"It's not so much the work
I enjoy," said the cabby,
"It's the people I run into."

My old Dad said I'd never make an accountant.

"There are three kinds of people in this world, son," he said. "Those who can count, and those who can't!"

An Irish handyman went down to the hardware store for some bolts.

"How long do you want them?" enquired the salesman.

"Well, to tell you the truth," replied the handyman, "I was sort of hoping to keep them."

Seasoned couple at the airlines reservations counter: "Two tickets to wherever our luggage is going."

GLOSSARY OF
MANAGEMENT TERMS

Ambitious:

Ruthless

Fred was an atheist, but he gave up. He said there were no holidays.

What would you call a woman who always knows where her husband is?

A widow.

The boss demanded to know where he had been.

"I've been for a haircut."

"You can't have your hair cut in office time!"

"Why not? It grows in office time."

"Not all of it," said the boss.

"So I didn't get it all cut off," he replied.

How many psychiatrists does it take to change a light bulb?

Only one. But the bulb must want to be changed.

GLOSSARY OF MANAGEMENT TERMS

Analytical Projection:

Guess

"I would go to the end of the world for you," he said.

"Yes, but would you stay there?" she yawned.

A young man looking for a job travelled to the country and approached the general store in a small town. The man behind the counter was also the president of the county football league and offered the lad a job immediately.

"We need a centre-half forward with courage and a strong set of hands," he said.

"Sorry sir," said the lad. "I don't know a thing about football."

"No worries. We need umpires too."

The butler was interviewing a prospective maid for the household and asked the girl for her references. She began rummaging around in her handbag. "I am afraid I've lost my reference from the Dorchester," she said, "but I've got these two spoons with the Dorchester crest to prove I worked there."

A bloke who was run over by the mobile library began to groan and moan. The librarian jumped out of the vehicle, bent down and said, "SSSShhhhhh!"

He had a stereo system
in his car for years.
His wife in the front and
her mother in the back.

GLOSSARY OF
MANAGEMENT TERMS

Deficiency Analysis:
Search for scapegoat

The club president was delivering his annual report and was praising the committee. "Unlike other clubs where half the committee does all the work and the other half are hopeless, here, it is completely the reverse!"

The judge fixed him with a beady eye. "How could you take money from people who trusted you?"

"Because it just doesn't work with people who don't trust you," the con man replied.

A bed is where one good turn can get all the blankets.

She stopped in front of the blind man and dropped all her small change into his cup with a clunk.

"God bless you, lady," he said. "I knew you was kind hearted the moment I saw you turn the corner."

GLOSSARY OF
MANAGEMENT TERMS

Deficit:
Staggering loss

She approached the hairdresser. "What do you have for grey hair?"

"The greatest respect, madam," he replied.

The customs officer at the airport asked Paddy if he had anything to declare.

"No, only this bottle of holy water from Lourdes."

The officer was interested and asked to see it.

When Paddy produced it the officer removed the cork and put his nose to the bottle.

"That's not water," he said grimly. "That's whisky."

"Mother of God!" exclaimed Paddy, "It's another bloomin' miracle!"

Fred's wife rang the cricket club.

"Sorry, he has just walked to the crease. He is about to bat. Shall I ask him to ring you back?"

"No. I'll hang on," she said.

"Good grief, you've got the biggest cavity I've ever seen, said the dentist. "You've got the biggest cavity I've ever seen."

"Okay," said the patient, "you don't have to repeat it."

"I didn't" said the dentist. "That was the echo!"

Diplomacy is when you make your in-laws feel at home, when you wish they were.

GLOSSARY OF MANAGEMENT TERMS

Delayed:

Forgotten

"The doctor told me to take these pills for the rest of my life."

"So, what's the problem?"

"He only gave me half a dozen."

If your wife insists on learning to drive, don't stand in her way.

The owner of a small business was telling his bank manager that the recession was tough. "Things are so bad that even people who don't pay have stopped buying."

"Education has failed the younger generation," said the businessman. "Our survey shows that as many as 40 per cent can't read, another 40 per cent can't write and the other 30 per cent can't add up."

GLOSSARY OF
MANAGEMENT TERMS

Delegate:
Pass the buck

"I have been asked to get married hundreds of times," she pouted.

"By whom?" he asked.

"My mum and dad," she said.

The doctor told his patient he had some bad news, and some very bad news.

"What's the bad news?"

"You've only got two weeks to live."

"What news can be worse than that?" cried the patient.

"I should have told you a fortnight ago."

Fred was trying to join the local team. "Have you had any experience?" asked the captain.

"Well, I think I once played with Don Bradman."

"Really?"

"Yes," said Fred, "he told me after the game who he was. He said if I was a batsman, he was Don Bradman."

The ship's purser asked the sailor how he had spent his month's pay on shore leave.

"Some went on drink, some on women. And I guess I squandered the rest," was the reply.

"What's a monologue, Dad?"

"That's a conversation with your mother, son."

Marriage begins as you sink in his arms, and ends with your arms in the sink.

GLOSSARY OF
MANAGEMENT TERMS

Environmental Pollution:
Other people's waste

It was so cold the other day that the local flasher was seen describing himself to a woman.

What do you call a man who has lost 90 per cent of his brain?

A widower.

After six months at Gamblers Anonymous, Fred believed he was cured. "I'd like to thank you all for helping me kick the habit," he said. "I'll never gamble again. In fact, I'd wager a fortune on it."

A gardener is a bloke
who calls a spade a spade;
until he falls over one.

GLOSSARY OF MANAGEMENT TERMS

Extreme Urgency:
Blind panic

Funny how man blames fate for all accidents, yet claims full responsibility for a hole in one.

The smart husband thinks twice before saying nothing.

"That was the best innings I've ever played."

"Well, you mustn't let that discourage you."

"I am not playing my best game today,"

"Really, what other games do you play?"

My mother-in-law has a speech impediment.

Now and then she has to pause for breath.

He used to be an
all-round athlete.

Now he's just all round.

GLOSSARY OF MANAGEMENT TERMS

Forecast:

Guess

The lovers were entwined in passionate embrace on the lounge floor when suddenly a car was heard coming up the driveway.

"Quick!" the woman shrieked. "That will be my husband. He's a policeman and he's twice as big as you."

Her companion hopped about frantically and said, "Where's the back door?"

"We haven't got one," she replied.

"Well, tell me quickly," he said, "where would you like one?"

My brother was known as
the Van Gogh of the violin.
He had no ear for it.

People who say they are going on a diet are just wishful shrinkers.

GLOSSARY OF MANAGEMENT TERMS

Frank Discussion:

Bloody argument

"I don't think I look 35, do you?" she asked her husband.

"No, I don't," he said, "but you used to."

An Englishman boarded a train with a large shaggy dog and sat opposite an Irishman.

Paddy looked at the dog for a while then said, "And what type of dog would that be?"

The surly Englishman replied, "It's a cross between an ape and an Irishman."

Paddy was quick with his reply, "You mean it's related to both of us!"

When Fred's house burned down he went off to the insurance company and demanded his compensation money, but he was soon to learn that the company didn't operate that way.

"It is our policy to replace your house and anything else you lost exactly in the same style and condition," said the manager.

"Hell," said Fred. "In that case I would like to cancel the policy I took out on my mother-in-law."

A man who says his wife can't take a joke, forgets himself.

GLOSSARY OF MANAGEMENT TERMS

Industrial By-Product:

Waste

“That’s a nice suit you are wearing. I wonder if the style will ever come back in fashion?”

The boss told the applicant there was a vacancy for a responsible worker. "Are you responsible?" he asked.

"I'm the right bloke alright," said Fred. "Every job I've had, when anything happened, everybody said I was responsible!"

Two husbands were leaning on the bar:

"Did you give your wife a lecture on economy like I told you?"

"Yes, I certainly did."

"And what was the result?"

"I've got to give up smoking."

It was the day of the grand final when the officials took a call from the gatekeeper. "There are two life-members here. They are close friends of the umpire and they have lost their tickets."

"Throw them out," said the executive. "They are liars. Whoever heard of an umpire having two friends!"

GLOSSARY OF MANAGEMENT TERMS

Long-Range Forecast:
Wild guess

He always wanted to be a comedian, but he was afraid people might laugh at him.

A small boy was watching his mother do the washing.

"Mum, where did you work before you got this job here with us?"

"Have you ever been cross-examined before?" asked the judge.

"Yes, your honour," replied the defendent. "I'm a married man."

Education is what you get from reading the fine print.

Experience is what you get from not reading it.

She said she can tell by looking at your husband's face if he is lying.

"Yes," she said. "If his lips are moving, he's lying."

Marriage has its good side. It teaches you loyalty, forbearance, self-restraint, and many other qualities you wouldn't need if you stayed single.

GLOSSARY OF MANAGEMENT TERMS

Pending:
Haven't figured it out yet

The wife was nervous as she got behind the wheel of their new car for the first time. "I hardly know what to do," she said.

"Just imagine I'm driving," he replied.

My mother-in-law thinks I'm effeminate.

But compared to her I probably am.

"Why do you keep coming home three parts sloshed?" demanded his wife.

"Because I keep running out of money!" replied her husband.

"Waiter, what's the difference between the steak and the hamburger?"

"About one day, sir."

GLOSSARY OF
MANAGEMENT TERMS

Profit Before Tax:
Loss

A neighbour is a person who listens to you attentively, through a wall.

Fred was explaining to his mate at the bar that he had had yet another fight with his mother-in-law. "But at least she came crawling to me on her hands and knees this time," he said.

His mate was impressed, "Why, what did she say?"

"Come out from under the bed, you pathetic, snivelling little coward and I'll clobber you again!"

At the press conference the boring politician droned along on his dreary speech, ad nauseam, until one reporter, a little the worse for drink, actually threw a bottle at him.

Unfortunately it missed the politician and hit another journalist a glancing blow on the head, to which his immediate response was, "Hit me again, I can still hear the bugger!"

Newspapers are still credible, provided you read between the lies.

GLOSSARY OF MANAGEMENT TERMS

Scheduled:

Hoped for

"I got rid of that rear noise in the car."

"How?"

"I made her sit in the front with me."

A father asked his son, "Why are you wearing my raincoat?"

His son replied, "Well, you don't want your best suit to get wet, do you?"

Said the drunk as he staggered into the kitchen:

"Am I home darling?"

In the orchestra he plays piano. At home he plays second fiddle.

GLOSSARY OF
MANAGEMENT TERMS

Shrewd:
Devious

An elderly spinster approached the pearly gates and knocked. "Who is it?" asked St Peter.

"It is I," came the reply.

"Oh no," muttered St Peter. "Not another school teacher."

The only thing wrong with political jokes is that they get elected.

She had served him so many burnt offerings that on their first anniversary he bought her an altar cloth.

The unionist on holiday sent a postcard home:

"HAVING A LOVELY TIME-AND-A-HALF."

They say he married her because her aunt left her a fortune. He hotly denies it, and says he would have married her whoever left her the fortune.

No woman ever shot her husband while he was doing the dishes.

GLOSSARY OF
MANAGEMENT TERMS

Strategy:
Low cunning

Capitalism: You possess two cows. You sell one and buy a bull.

Socialism: You possess two cows. You give one of them to your neighbour.

Communism: You possess two cows. The government confiscates them and provides you with milk.

NAZISM: *You possess two cows. The government confiscates them and shoots you.*

EUROPEAN COMMON MARKET: *You possess two cows. The government confiscates them, shoots one, milks the other and pours it down the drain.*

"Doctor, doctor," said the patient as he burst into the psychiatrist's room, "I feel invisible."

"I'm sorry, I can't see you now."

Cabinet decided to adjourn business for a dinner break and they trouped into the parliamentary restaurant. The prime minister ordered a mixed grill.

"And what about your vegetables?" asked the waiter.

"Oh, they can order what they like," he replied.

GLOSSARY OF
MANAGEMENT TERMS

Supplementary Statistical Information:
Padding

Sales resistance is the triumph of mind over patter.

Fred was talking to his mate in the pub. "The wife is shopping crazy. She will buy absolutely anything marked down. Yesterday she came home with an escalator."

SIGN AT A CREEK:

"When this sign is under water the crossing is dangerous."

"Congratulations, my boy," said the groom's uncle. "I'm sure you will look back on today as the happiest day of your life."

"But I'm not getting married until tomorrow," protested the lad.

"I know," said the uncle.

The shop steward addressed the workers. "From now on all wages are doubled, holidays extended to six months and we shall only work on Fridays."

From the back of the hall came the retort, "What, every bloody Friday?"

An atheist is a man with no invisible means of support.

GLOSSARY OF
MANAGEMENT TERMS

Terminal Payment:
Golden handshake

The patient told the psychiatrist, "Everybody hates me."

He replied, "Don't be silly. Everyone hasn't met you yet."

The cab driver finally gave the job up.

He didn't like people talking behind his back.

"Waiter, why does this chicken have one leg missing?"

"It was in a fight."

"Well, take it away and bring me the winner."

The advertisement for a kitchen gadget said it was so marvellous it would cut the housework in half. So she bought two.

GLOSSARY OF MANAGEMENT TERMS

Urgency:
Panic

SIGN IN PUB:

"If you are drinking to forget, please pay for your drinks in advance."